*S*KY

CHRISTOPHER BUCKLEY

SKY

THE SHEEP MEADOW PRESS
RIVERDALE-ON-HUDSON, NEW YORK

All inquiries and permission requests should be addressed to:
    The Sheep Meadow Press
    P. O. Box 1345
    Riverdale-on-Hudson, NY 10471

Designed and typeset by S.M.
Distributed by The University Press of New England.

Printed on acid-free paper in the United States. This book meets the guidelines for permanence and durability of the Committee on Production Guidelines for Book Longevity of the Council on Library Resources.

Author photo by Nadya Brown.

Library of Congress Cataloging-in-Publication Data

Buckley, Christopher, 1948-
  Sky / Christopher Buckley.
      p. cm.
  ISBN 1-931357-22-6
  I. Title.
  PS3552.U339S55 2004
  811'.54--dc22

                           2004011175

and sky above, which after a while I saw was
the root to what I suffered from . . .

— Gerald Stern

ACKNOWLEDGEMENTS:

Thanks to the National Endowment for the Arts for a grant for 2001 which enabled me to write many of these poems.

These poems first appeared—sometimes in other versions—in the following journals to whose editors grateful acknowledgement is due:

Crazyhorse: Desert Song
FIELD: Poem After Lu Yu
5 am: Cloud Study; Paris Dispatch; Unhappiness
HUBBUB: Stars Above Fresno: The Resurrection, Cookham
The Journal: Five Days Rain
LUNA: For Ernesto Trejo in the Other World; Or Not
Natural Bridge: Poem Freely Accepted from the Polish
Pleiades: Imperfect Contrition; A Little Poem About God; Sky
Poetry International: Old News
Poet Lore: Voyage to the Great Attractor
Quarterly West: On a Painting by Wen Jai; In Fresno, I'm Living in My Dreams
Rivendell: Dispatch from Santa Barbara
Smartish Pace: A Pair of Shoes (Een Paar Schonen); Philosophical Poem on the Usual Subjects
Third Coast: All This Time
Tiferet: Mederranean Clouds
TriQuarterly: Cloud Journal; Physics & the Secret of Nothing

Thanks to Nadya Brown for enduring support. Thanks to Gary Soto for help and friendship. Special thanks to Gary Young and Jon Veinberg for tireless editing and revision suggestions.

CONTENTS

I

A LITTLE POEM ABOUT GOD

Inventor of trees, a first draft of the vast prairies,
      He was looking for something
           to direct our attention.

After a while, He specialized in birds, the light
      analogies He hoped we'd pick up on
           before they all disappeared.

And though you'd think birds alone would have
      kept him busy, He became distracted
           with the seas, the metaphor

of the blue and the invisible, the indeterminate
      at every turn, the absolute subterfuge
           of stars—all the possibilities

like currency, until there we were, wealthy beyond
      belief, with our free will and philosophies.
           But in time we grew heavy

with Time, and the sea was turquoise, green, or grey,
      and there was no disposition, no indication
           in the white caps or the breeze.

Occasionally, the moon traced a finger along the shore,
      and we had at least, sand in common—one of the last
           things slated to wear away.

A cloud hoists the sky on its back. He looks out the window
      again from his great room of clouds—at some
           old light, at weariness gathered

in the cypress or cedar boughs, in the arms of the wind.
Waves carry us out toward the stars, but we
are not built for eternity—we only

appreciate things we are going to lose, or have lost . . .
funny thing about human nature—we have to decide
every day what to do with our lives.

In memory of Yehuda Amichai

ALL THIS TIME

Fifty-two years have passed

like the turning of a palm . . .
— Charles Wright

I want to point to a horizon so scoured with light that I might forget
that it's only dust

That makes it blue, so easily blurred, so immediate with a longing
too available to us all.

Despite the various and sundry heavens, there is no light I resemble.
Still, I can't be the only one

Sifting through the old objections amid the recurrent incongruities
of air. I swear I can still hear

My stepmother saying, "Hang the expense, Agnes, throw the cat
another goldfish!" Our fortunes

So entwined out there among the dark, who on earth could know?
My mind's sky is still full

Of the same poor birds, full of clouds inscribed with the lost alphabet
of the Phoenicians, their sails

Like capital Ss I practiced in penmanship throughout grammar school,
through the early Middle Ages.

I've got my hand in memory's back pocket trying to recall when I was 8,
high in a tree, sailing over the valley.

I'd open a fist and white feathers would fly from my hands,
sentimental sprays of stardust

I didn't know belonged to Longfellow and Whittier, would soothe me.
                    I may have expanded

The details a bit, but something was burning its way out
                    of my skin, some semi-

Mystical photochemical processes that felt as relentless,
                    as imperishable as the sea,

That left me fearing next to nothing for a while, my arms full
                    as they were of wild nasturtiums,

Fennel, or sage whenever I closed my eyes out beyond the dark
                    shoulders of the border oaks.

And somehow I found my way through the deep woods to here,
                    though I possessed nothing

That resembled courage or approximated agile thought, heading out
                    each day across the street

Or into the hills, where—much as I do now arriving each morning
                    for work—I wore a hat, a vest,

A tin star pinned above my heart, all of which demonstrated my undying
                    devotion, my patience and puzzled

Attachment to the skies, though it's likely that there is still no God
                    who needs my steadfast thoughts.

IN FRESNO, I'M LIVING IN MY DREAMS

my early 30s, alone in one of those old spacious hardwood homes
       with the porch and cement pillars, two foot–wide

strips of cement running into the carport, grass coming up
       summer green in between, in the shade of the overhang.

I'm standing at the kitchen sink, looking out the window on nothing,
       faucet running, dishes piled on the linoleum counter . . .

and then the phone rings in the dark world of 5 a.m. Someone from
       another time zone, a town in Ohio, tells me my Aunt Veleska,

who we all called Babe, has died. Last relative on my father's side
       who, for the past five years, has had no idea where she is,

who had a feeding tube on the advice of the good doctors until
       benefits ran out and they no longer wanted to keep her

alive, as was her clear wish when she stopped eating, miserable
       as her mind surely was. It must have been a calm blast

of light to at last be untied from the long project of suffering, like
       a fissured vase finally breaking, the water rushing out,

evaporating. And this leaves me the only one who knows any of us
       were ever here. Even in the dark I could briefly see

her face as I remember it as a boy-her wine-red lips, black curled hair,
       fox stole and felt gloves as they had them in the '50s.

I saw the dim mahogany light of her big brick house before I went
       off to bed in my pajamas with the snaps and feet,

saw how happy she was with Bernie, sitting there in the dim silence
of the living room, of the Midwest, with two tall glasses

of Rhinegold. That was almost the life, as they could never marry,
she being divorced and Catholic and doing what everyone

else thought they should, and praying regularly to end up some place
beyond the grey confines of Ohio, like my father

who went west and discovered California and never returned, he
being so close all his life to becoming a crooner,

a matinee idol, in his mind. For all that, he died as unknown as
his mother who outlived everyone on her funeral list

of invitees except Babe. Today, not one is left to throw a grey flower
into the flat lap of Ohio in her lonely mis-blessed memory,

to say So Long the way no one does anymore.... I go back to sleep,
to Fresno, to the kitchen where I turn the counter radio

to the memories station. The girl who lives next door drives up and
steps out of her car, back from a trip to the coast, tosses

her long brassy pony tail side to side as she hoses off the glistening
dust and sand near the lacy shade of the pepper tree,

where I look out to the blistering blue, where I see a bird pumping
its wings like a hand waving in the anonymous distance,

where there is a vapor trail, and one silver cloud loose in the arms
of the wind. The second hand on my water-proof watch

sweeps through time—I'm living again, happily in the Tower District,
near the park and pitiful zoo, the sad music store and

Italian deli just up Olive street, not quite half of everything that will
        happen, or not happen to me, has passed, suspended

in the afternoon's brown light, in this other life. I am content
        knowing so little, young enough beneath a blank sky

to hold the washrag, keeping a firm grip, stacking the dishes, all white
        and even as souls, everyone in Ohio, and Fresno, still alive...

VOYAGE TO THE GREAT ATTRACTOR

> *...our Milky Way galaxy and its neighbors are moving*
> *toward a Great Attractor—a distant continent of matter,*
> *mostly invisible, containing thousands of galaxies.*
> — Alan Dressler, *Voyage to the Great Attractor*

Bless me by the immobile sea again, that I can stand here
                    sightless beyond the sun,

Travelling in my mind. I'm not going anywhere, really,
                    never moving far from

My starting point-the problem before me, as always, encrypted
                    beyond the parochial air

Burning down into my hands as if this were all of it-
                    water or atmosphere . . . .

                              *

The sky is in no hurry to reconnoiter, the ocean in no rush
                    to offer hints beyond

The residual certificates of salt. Here we have only the unsolved
                    blue on hand, while,

In one sense, passing 50, I was sure there was something I knew
                    about the sky, some

Response holding steady before the recurrent clouds reflecting
                    the usual indigence

Here below, the way the waves wash endlessly the memory
                    of sea foam from the sand.

*

And so all around us, a cosmos in flight, grains and flecks,
                         ellipses and strings of light

Sloshing about like blood cells in an enlarged heart. In the last
                         century we have moved

From the center of the universe to a distant outpost in our own
                         unassuming galaxy – our neighbors

And every bit of ice and iron in the area are red-shifted and pulled
                         towards a body of thousands of galaxies,

Great unseeable wodges of Dark Matter, concentrating the light, calling
                         us all in far beyond any star

Or star wall we know. Sinking among our own small matters, we are
                         displaced from wherever it is

We were-blind fish, wobbly, glittering riffs, incremental through
                         the black, breathless, expanse,

Encountering the apparent nothing that awaits – or doesn't wait –
                         for us all. The hosanna choruses

Of our individual atoms gripping together for the time being,
                         but falling so predictably

Short in the long run that we would no doubt do well to look for more
                         immediate images/concerns.

*

The image first came to Einstein at sixteen – what would it be like
                    to ride a beam of light? And thus,

Age relative to speed. Every second the earth is struck by 4 & 1/2
                    pounds of sunlight, but hardly slows

Down, each quark spun along with us, each weightless theory.
                    We knew God's shoe size but

Next to nothing about particle physics when the angels began
                    to ignore us for good.

                              *

And always in dreams I drift back home – that little constellation
                    of thought still spinning

Brightly above Montecito's trees, the laundry-fresh clouds stained
                    at the edges, sepia outlines

Clearly and forever cut out of the past . . . Peter Pan lunch pail
                    with red plastic handle,

The slow grammatical hours of the day until we are let out
                    at 3:00, and I decide to walk

Rather than ride the bus so I can talk to kids as I remember them.
                    I go up to Stanton Richards –

To whom I haven't spoken in 30 years – and ask, "How are you? What
                    do you do with your time?"

And time dissolves at Our Lady of Mt. Carmel School... my first day
                    of Second grade, sitting behind

The class rooms during lunch with a few kids in the orbiting shade
of palms and acacias – some of us

Wearing the uniform grey and blue shirts or dresses, some in T-shirts
or street clothes, not that anyone cares.

I am happy simply to have friends to eat my lunch with, to look
into the dark sparkling eyes

Of the little Mexican girl next to me as we lean against a large
sandstone rock, as she looks up

After the invisible stars, invisible heaven, after fair weather clouds,
each of us holding half a sandwich,

Bread white as clouds, as stars – and I ask, I guess, about our lunch break,
"How long do we have?"

TO ERNESTO TREJO IN THE OTHER WORLD

Still tonight, the stars are where we left them,
nonchalant, incontestable in their distance.

Once we were those stars — all of us atoms
no memory will admit. And once it mattered

what we made of stars, and read into the sky;
but now all the theories scatter like blackbirds

from a field, there, against the unrequited blue.
I have no idea, truly, where you are — dry wind

in eucalyptus, sedan of clouds pearl-edged in the west.
The soul could well be that cloud in the empty shape

of clouds given the spare charities of Time, the breeze
that sweeps any of us away. I wonder if you see

the winos who never left The Eagle Café, the solar systems
of grease spinning on the blue plate specials, if you can

see Spain, a country you never knew? Speculation is
you overlook it all, can look down *Diagonal* or out 46,

stone-blazing afternoons in Madera or *Madrid*, or in
Barcelona, the evening walking bejeweled into the bay.

In Fresno, I remember only one guitar that spoke
of the sea, and a cypress or two along Van Ness,

and no sea of course, no Ramblas with caged birds
reciting in their paradisiacal tongues, no dusty angels

high in the sycamores who, if they could, would descend
for a drink at one of the chrome tables in the shade.

So many gone now, who knows if you could meet anyone
on Olive Street and praise the poets of Spain?

We never spoke of the Alhambra, the refrain of waves
at Castelldefels, the lost continents of the moon.

Whatever is out there is here, just as well. And so
I think of Rome where Giordano Bruno proclaimed

a plurality of worlds, a belief I almost maintain,
excepting the examinations by iron and fire.

And so crows today are just crows, happy to hop about
suburban lawns without an inner life. This is the world

and it all happens here – nothing else stands for the sky,
weak and frayed as it is with our conjecture. Nevertheless,

I accede to the a lyric mantilla of stars, a mythopoeic light
filtering down far stanzas of the dark as evidence,

perhaps, of hope. There is no other light, and we have
gone through eons worth of it with less and less to show.

Is there any way, my friend, to tell us where we are
headed tonight? I cannot see beyond Miramar Point,

that small shore of childhood where I was content
with the omnipotent salt air, with the mocking bird

impromptu in the pines, where I stand, feet in the cold
sand, a tide rising, the sea reflecting the clear light

of space back into space – the anaphora of the heart
holding on before God, or light, or none of the above.

MEDITERRANEAN CLOUDS
— Es Castell, Menorca

> *The Big Empty is also a subject of some note,*
> *Dark, dark and never again...*
> — Charles Wright

Clouds on a string in the west,
                        spelling out
their blank predicament,
                        marshalling no argument
against the dark
                we're headed for.
Bits of Styrofoam
                bob on the swells,
                                the sun
shakes out its dreams in dust
                        and was dreaming
of dust all along....
                We've read the certifications
of the dead,
                we've made our calculations in the air
and turned
                out here before the waves
                                with little more
than the detachment,
                        the blandishments of daylight
grazing our cheeks.
                Earlier each day
the sky calls in its debts,
                        the insolvency of our hearts —
the fog unspools,
                so this can't help but be another poem
about the soul....

*

Outside Bar Miramar, on the *Calla Fonts*,

you sit

with an *Estrella*, you sit with your life

like the light blue

spaces shifting off with the apostasy

of clouds,

with crumbs blowing off the plate

of bread and oil

and olives.

You watch the jumping fish rise

out of the bay,

the first edge of moon,

both silver...

you accept these

compensations,

the small salvations

of late afternoon, the fair weather

clouds reflecting

the comparative poverties

of the past, tattered shirts

on a rooftop line....

But this is the new life

of the spirit –

shopping for wine or onions,

a potato omelet

in the bar by the bay.

Let the stars starve in the dark

with their bright hexagrams

and prescience,

their persistence after death

with or without us....

At the mouth of the harbor

the buoy lights
　　　　　　　set against the sky
　　　　　　　　　　　　　　might be stars
just as well.

*

Sit here by the pittosporum and marguerites
　　　　　　　　　　　　　　　　with me
and think —
　　　　　　St. Augustine came to aggravate us
with sin,
　　　　　　and our simple desire
　　　　　　　　　　　　　　for the earth,
to remind us about the soul
　　　　　　　　　　　　and the unreliable
veil of the senses,
　　　　　　　　and offered that we should not
expect evidence
　　　　　　for what is beyond
us in the first place.
　　　　　　　　　　　Long before the stars
or galaxies,
　　　　　　the universe held the lightless seed
of our every atom,
　　　　　　　　unbreathing and flat, without
dreams.
　　　　　　And before that, what?
　　　　　　　　　　　　　What bright threads
up the long stem of the dark?
　　　　　　　　　　　What resemblance
might instruct us?

Sunset, and St. Augustine
is peeling an orange,
                    and the tiny spray of acid
breaking from the peel
                    gives off the brilliance
of the Spanish coast
                    burning above Valencia,
                                        of the world
he has defamed,
                    having grown old in it.
                                        The light
of this world surely is the light
                    of the other....

                              *

The sun's burden settles
                    on palm leaves
feathered out
          by an inconsequential wind ...
nothing stands
          in place of the world,
                         although Byzantine
mystic Nicophorus the Solitary
                    told us, "Attention
is the appeal of the soul to itself."
                         though the palms
gaze indifferently out to sea,
                    though there is no escaping
the stars.

          In your notebook, you again take up the passage
about the passing
              and glory of the world –

                                        (you've kept track –
more passing than glory).
                        The sparrows await more
crumbs and do not commiserate
                                about mortality-
in the chair across from you, you have
                                the soft light of October
and the little schismatics
                        in their cheerful waistcoats
do not put one day
                before another,
                                do not find the handiwork
of the infinite in clouds.
                        It's all you need to breathe
out with evening and accept
                                your inconsequence
among the thistles and marguerites.
                                Never mind
the circumstantial accounts,
                        the refined grist of scholarship –
the theory
                never the thing itself.
                                The field larks sing
for the sky,
                the preamble
                        of light tumbling
                                in their blood,
still in their pebble-sized hearts.
                                Brush strokes on the horizon,
the imponderable
                backdrop of air.
                                The birds suggest,
it is impudent to question
                what we're given
                                before the dark,

20

what thin intimations spin away

                just over our heads —

what clues dissolve against the blue,

                or just hold vaguely on,

like a little mist, almost overlooked,

                and offered up

on the salt-white light

           off the sea....

UNHAPPINESS

> *The reconnaissance planes and God*
> *Will never know*
> *What we really want*
> — Amichai

Above me, the birds have been talking all morning
        and haven't called one thing into question.

Everything we desire does us in, but I shouldn't take
        it personally, looking out on the ocean,

On the past dissolving, no more than salt in the waves.
        I should be a small breeze through

The coral trees, leaving the shining aspects of the world
        to their own devices. Yet I am still perplexed

By Neitzche – not by his brilliance, his life-long despair,
        but by the story of him at the end, going mad,

Confronting a horse in the street and asking, "My God,
        why are we so unhappy?" I've never understood

Whether he recognized the horse as God and demanded
        an answer, or whether he simply saw the horse

As a fellow being, full of suffering? Under the same stars
        we cannot find one corollary for happiness

Satisfactory to us all. If it were only a matter of prayer,
        of just asking, we would have everything,

And so little conflict then across the historical plains,
        Fewer records of gangs riding into town

On little ponies saying, "We're taking over!" The beaches
   would reflect us, bathed with an aureate grace.

What a lot of bald petitioners we've been, always thinking
   we deserve something more than our lives

Beneath the sky – more glitz, a little rococo, a carnival
   parading with the rich through the new snow,

A small coffee in a smart café, a cinematic alternative
   to the soul. More talent, a sound-byte in the spot light,

And who would know me then? Since childhood, I've been
   trying to take my cue from the trees-but they seem

To still be listening for something far away—each evening
   I hear them murmuring about birds that have left.

But anymore, I am not to be trusted when it comes to birds-
   the least of them offering a capsule of joy,

Asking nothing in return, and all our lives we've been hoarding
   everything in sight. Now I'm content to just have

My blood pumping acceptably through my veins, and not
   bursting like a thunder cloud. And like us

The trees look up to the bright scrawl and hieroglyphics
   of God each night, or the star-flecked mimesis

Of the ocean. What are we going to do about our lives now,
   softening steadily out there like the summer fog,

Fading slowly back out to sea? Here or there, a landscape
   in grey—a gold or russet leaf to catch the eye

Of someone just as often appeased with nothing more
    than the morning's entablature of clouds,

Ordered as God's lost thoughts—as if they were available,
    and he had been thinking of us, all along.

ETERNITY
(being a condensed spiritual and aesthetic biography)
for VS

No one says I look 55 – no one says I don't, except my new friend
Virgil. He has two Catholic daughters and like me, hates to fly, but
there's no other way to get home in time for the youngest's 1st
Communion. I almost remember mine... I've been scared ever since
– of Death, of course. You tell me why.... In 2nd grade, the nun lec-
tured us about Eternity, which almost arrived later from Cuba in the
early '60s, Cuba where my friend Virgil was born, which has at least
one entrance to hell and exits in Spain and L.A. In the afterlife, I
don't think anyone is rolling cigars while someone reads them Don
Quixote in the original. Anyway, we were going to spend Eternity in
hell if we did not do as we were told. Sister explained that Eternity
was like an enormous steel ball, the size of the earth, upon which an
eagle, gliding in from the cosmic starry dark beyond Cleveland and
the east coast, once every million years, landed and took off again.
The time it took that steel ball to completely wear away from the
friction of the eagle landing and lifting away was less than a second
of Eternity, the time we'd be burning on a hot rock for cussing, eat-
ing hot dogs on Fridays, not making our yearly Easter obligation of
communion and mass, or having impure thoughts about Belinda
Sanchez. Go figure.

What if, on the practical side, the universe – and so time-
space – does curve back on itself like a huge quesadilla? We're going
nowhere. What, then, have we been suffering for all along? More
specifically, what have I been doing with that image like a fish hook
in my brain for 48 years? Nuns, with their psycho-spiritual hammer-
locks, were terrorists, and they did not discriminate among ages or
ethnic groups. Death, darkness, and sure damnation were there equal-
ly for us all if we didn't stop talking during mass and go out and fina-
gle quarters from relatives and folks on our block for the pagan
babies. Dear God.

I don't know what angel brings me these lines in the middle of the night after I'm up and down the hall to the bathroom, brings them every few years like a palm tree and a pool of water appearing after sands have shifted for no reason, like some metaphysical crust of light. Some angel sweeping down with dust, one in the back of the chorus singing hosannas like nobody's business who has a little time to spare, an angel who every now and then hands off a few imagistic granules while I'm flaming away here in the flesh, in darkness where I might not know the source but would know a gift when I heard one.

Once I'm half awake and the cells are ticking over like new stars, I lose track of time and switch the lamp on and off and write down phrases, losing sleep – what does it come to? The door of a '59 Chevy swings open like a vault and lets out some earlier, more sprightly version of me, only a few blocks from happiness, or the sea, which ever comes first – with my papers and a new poem in hand – more than I arrived with. Who knew where I was headed? The nuns were sure: Hell. Virgil and I voted for Spain, even southern California if that's the best we could do to breathe cool salt air. Maybe I could do this forever, who knows? As I was taught, worse things could happen to me. Outside of Time, will poems matter? Why ask now – I'm not an academic, an administrator, slick in a Republican suit. We're not for long, not forever. Death, of course. And next? I hope it's not hell, or anywhere near Pennsylvania, where I already served ten years for my sins.

Dear God. Thank you for the gift of the eccentric brain, this associative jelly. Thank you for this moonraking poem which keeps me alive in prayer, in doubt, and in hope. This poem which for once did not take 5 months and 50 drafts, though I would have waited patiently as always – like salt dissolving from the sea, like air gathering to be somewhere else, like the last flake of rust outside of time....

II

OLD NEWS: POEM ON A BIRTHDAY

Whatsoever of it has flown away is past;
Whatsoever of it remains is future.
— St. Augustine, *Confessions, XI*

When it came down to it, I loved the '50s, the spectacular black
    and white winter nights, starlight dusting down

Shiny and crystalline as phenobarbital, a fleet of drowsy angels
    drifting over the car lots and department stores

As I waited in the front seat of the old Pontiac for my father
    to come out of the radio station, the call letters

Over the door humming their pink neon like a distant nebula.
    Now at 55, grey matter drying up like the river-

Bank clay it really is, I can still recognize a young Sinatra,
    on "Street of Dreams," and see the white hot dog

wrappers fluttering along the foul line at Ebbets Field on TV,
    and the grey phrasing of that soft lost light.

I was sure then that the slow progress of days was in my debt,
    that I was due some great fate or adulation

For just breathing in style among my friends, for we started out
    thinking we knew all that was hidden in the air –

Where, perhaps, we were finally headed with our half dollar
    souls, like the star beam burning homeward

In the bird's breast, the salt glaze rising off the froth of waves
    in our image—less and less always in our arms.

*

These days, all of my friends are going to Italy — soon, every bit
    of the past we know will pass us by. Beneath

The umbrella pines, along the scored basalt road into the ruins,
    there are things I remember remembering there

Surely from another life — same air, same thick sun, familiar
    dust settling in the mind come evening, or

On the road through the Etruscan hill town, some deep
    blue tiles surrounding the fountain

One afternoon like pieces of the Aegean winking back?
    Either way, it's nice being here, sky thinning,

A cloud tipped over the sea like one of God's discarded
    helmets. Once I would have asked for help,

For the intercession of the winds to carry me off beyond
    the broken ankle of light at Point Conception,

But today it's enough to be next to nowhere in California,
    though in the photo on my desk I sit

With my grandfather on a crate in an orange grove
    in Florida, in 1950, the world looking fine

As far as I can see. I'm wearing shorts and a baseball cap,
    staring off into the horizon as if he were

Always going to be there and not just in the speechless light
    of a photograph, and not just in the approaching

Dark 50 years later — the grainy finish not picking up my
  tiny wings which will leave me, mid-air,

Before I'm seven. But that's me all the same, an orange
  in my hands, right leg shorter than the left —

Sun generous in winter there, a white sky, where no one knew
  what mattered as I was stupefied, too close

To the invisible impasse above me to interpret a time
  when everything was all already ours....

The dark flame-shaped leaves, daylight dividing the rows,
  rehearsing its comings and goings among

The living, I breathed the blue air and the sky looked
  right through us as if it were nothing,

Or we little more than that for wondering how we could
  ever be the stardust at the start of things.

STARS ABOVE FRESNO

Just outside of town
it's dark enough
to see the stars
no one is ever going to
visit.
        The sycamores and
crepe myrtle stand
for something in that
brown after–light
where we walked down
Arthur Street, Olive,
or Wishon.
            Knots of light,
a steadfast haze above
the arbors and midnight trees
that wouldn't clear
even in our twenties
when we finally drove off
into our lives....
                Surely
the dust still burns
over the roofs
as the sky ignites
with every irreconcilable
fact.
        Leaves swirl
among the stars, and
the soul, like any one
of them, is red–shifted
away from here,
from the business and
lies of the world,

from each bit
of love or trouble
we ever were.
                    Tonight,
the sky is clear –
I look out to where
everything has vanished....
Thirty years is nothing.

OR NOT
Vandenberg AFB, Lompoc, CA

The missile going off
shakes the house, the air
almost viscous as glass,
as we rush out to see
the stars swept back
and the hot nitrogen-
white plume cascade up,
launching Landsat 7
with digital imaging
that can isolate the sky-
blue pack of *Gauloises*
in a would-be Jean Paul
Belmondo's hand as he
leans against the digue
in Wimereux and lights-up
above the existential waves –
that can pick out the fact
that there's no Surgeon
General's warning printed
on the side.
                    But this –
young as he is, all the old
dangers passé – doesn't matter;
there are few secrets left
to keep away from death.
Now there's the invisible
stream of information
circumscribing the globe,
substantive as a con
trail, translucent at twilight –
now there's new light tilted
to a satellite so our SUVs

can be located with a flick
of a dashboard switch, a cellular
beep, and our tire repaired
tout de suite...
                    Once,
such rumbling and air defense
drills had me ducking
beneath my shaking desk —
blood gone cold, Khrushchev
pounding the UN table
with his belligerent shoe —
had me excused from French
in Catholic High to sit
alone in a bathroom stall,
two decades before 1984,
sweating out a future,
waiting for everything
I know to vaporize,
to turn back to sky.

DISPATCH FROM SANTA BARBARA, 2001

Mid-summer, July 4th in fact, but I'm not in town for the fireworks display from the breakwater. I'm here on errands, an emergency trip to the dentist, in and out before they crowd East Beach, Ledbetter, and the harbor, packing in on the sand thick as grunion under a phosphorescent moon.

I have an hour before I have to be somewhere, and I stop in Alameda Park where my mother first brought me as a child. There was a pool of shade under some trees and no swans drifting a little lake, no roses, no hedges in the shape of a heart – precious little except the wood bandstand that even then was no longer in use. Little but that block of shade – Anacapa to Santa Barbara Street, Micheltorena to Sola – courtesy of Morton Bay Figs and Spanish palms, and the creamy, book-perfect, fair-weather clouds of the '50s going over the Figueroa range – since age 4, the clouds and trees carrying off my thoughts....

And today I think of Thomas Wolfe, the sad line anyone knows about home. He knew about time, the quick dusty path here below the clouds. Perhaps he knew what was coming with real estate on the California Coast, way back when everyone lived in bungalows.... Now, making more money than I ever imagined, I am nonetheless dispossessed, can only afford to live an hour north in the wind and fog. I stand here, my feet on a sidewalk worn rough as beach sand, pavement I've walked off and on for 50 years, looking up to the blue or to the old clear stars, and it's hard to call it mine.

My work is 3 hours south of here, and so I'm driven, in all senses, past what I love. This morning, I'm taking time off from the world to be in it, to turn back – in star time – an instant, to 50 years ago when my mother took me after a nap out to the free, green republic of the park, from our turquoise stucco apartment on Micheltorena. We had just moved here and no one had heard of Santa Barbara, no one cared it was here an hour-and-a-half above L.A., a sleeping arboretum even angels overlooked, where we had next to nothing, and everything, where father worked nights, and my mother and I ate fried bologna and tomato soup in the Formica kitchen in front of a GE plastic radio. I had this life beneath the cool plush oaks and I didn't know to ask for anything more.

The Bandstand still standing...the small metal harp at the top, the cupboards for dwarfs all around underneath... the criss-cross walk corner to corner, the honorary wino in this black thrift store suit and white tennis shoes, smoking alone by the chained-off steps leading to the platform where I raced around in circles when I was 4...the 2 obligatory people passed out on the grass, newspapers over their faces, the early silent heavy air going by, slowly it seems....

Beneath the star pines and magnolias, the voluminous pittosporum, the 1 jacaranda pushing out for sun, the 5 paltry redwoods, the single eugenia grown exponentially beyond hedge size, older than me...I'm counting trees, so I keep it this time. And I want to name the St. Joseph's candle thrown out thick and twisted, to appeal to Our Lady of Sorrows with its washed-out pink walls and bell tower across the way, as if this, or any of these lost listings could help me reclaim or hold my home.

This park, this place, as full and spare as I remember it at 4 – no adornment but the leaves, the carved top of the picnic table, someone's initials sunk beneath the brown paint, from Catholic High up the street in 1954, the bare civic patches raked, and sprayed with a hose – part of the world that doesn't miss me, where, if I could, if I had more time, the simple wherewithal of dirt, I'd be here all my days, as content as the trees for all the sky to see – as the acorn woodpecker laughing at God, and at his own good fortune, at the same sparrows and rogue pack of pigeons claiming the earth or whatever is left of it here alongside the 1 picnic table and the grass as they peck at the grains of light. I join them again today, holding on to everything the wind has left to offer....

JESUS CHRIST RISING FROM THE DEAD IN COOKHAM
The Resurrection, Cookham –Stanley Spencer, 1924-26

Who would be born again
    only to live and die,
        in Cookham?

Only everyone ever known here –
    like weeds, like water
        hyacinths...

The least among you shall,
    nevertheless, rise,
        in a shiny suit,

In your white as pastry skin,
    sleep-walking up the low
        atmosphere,

Greeting your neighbors among
    the gossip of the unkempt
        mounds and stones

And river's edge – even the names
    of the dispossessed shall
        fill the wind...

Everyone on the dole for light.
    And the boatmen in their
        cloudy robes

Await them at the shore of all lost
    cares, radiant where
        the water waits

with the patience of stars — there
    to collect the watery souls —
        the coal man

And post mistress, the woman with
    the crocheted tea cozies
        in the jam shop,

The painter, the professor of bicycle
    parts, and the unemployed
        whistler after taxies,

The licker of butcher paper with
    the dogs — all called equally forth
        with a starry crown,

Kings and queens in housecoats
    And carpet slippers,
        in chapel-best

When Jesus raises his arms through
    the sooted air to call out
        the innocent,

Or mostly so, who have known the dull
    earth and the ordinary
        glory of the grass —

And thus they are beckoned forth, beyond
    the calm morning
        of Cookham,

the tow path, and river mists, the world,
    and the common infinity
        of the blue.

CLOUD STUDY

They overlook the details of this life —
witness the Wobblies, The Social Gospel,
the painters of those caves in Spain who hid
everything from the sky.
                              They turn their imposing
backs to us in disregard, the way we turn
from the dispossessed begging on the street,
our dull and unresponsive eyes
                              focused vaguely
on a future as unassailable as hope just over
the horizon. They could well be, it strikes me,
God's stand-ins, even forward observers
were there any interest
                              in every imaginable
affliction here below. But they testify to nothing,
sauntering away in their own cloud-time over
the nonrepresentational hills to the strains of
something as glum as Mahler
                              without the first
thought for any transgressions whatsoever
in the light, any aureate haze or least advertised
transformation at the end of the day.
                              Are we, then,
little more than dust, as the plants are dust, as dust
is dust? At a minimum, aren't we fellow travelers
with the impressionistic trees? The flint-shade
of poplars and beeches reaches out
                              with a river effect
from an old world, and sun flakes flash, revealing
the silver left-overs of wind — some of us brighter,
some staying a bit longer than others, in the slip-
stream, in the starless drifting.

ON A PAINTING BY WEN JAI

...the only ones who visit are drifting clouds.
— Han-Shan Te-Ch'ing
...but the clouds are too deep
to know where.
— Chia Tao

They were seeking

their lives –
in the ancient trees,

the shapes

that empty out
from wind

to fit the cliffs

like wind....
Windblown clouds,

pale cliffs

and mountain pinnacles
rising there –

the world ascends,

and they are
at the bottom

of a river gorge,

taking their steps
on the broken trail....

They are not dead –
their bodies move

beneath the sky,
and there is still

a long way

to go . . . .

★

Who would be
        Han-Shan now, or his friend Shih-Te,
living in the wild,
          wearing rags,
               scratching
a poem into bark,
          pecking lines into the rock face
then running away,

          giving up even that –
               having nothing,
only the whole world forever?

★

        California is long
as Wen Jai's hanging scroll,
          Immortals' Mountain
with Pavilions.
        Driving up and down

the coast
        we are like drifting clouds,
              light ink
on paper.
        This painting
          is not about us,
but about emptying
        the mind,
            that clay bowl
we go begging with.
        Some Buddhists say
the artless meditations

                                        of the air above
                                                        are all
          that should concern us,
                                    but not even Po Chu-i could
          resist praising
                          the green world,
                                              the river journey,
          the white cup of light
                                      in the high cliff window,
          the wine,
                          the evening
                                  leading to such a lost place,
          to the silences
                        in the mouth
                                      of the river gorge
          where we have left
                          almost everything behind.

          The pavilions
                        midway up look out
                                          on a path
          at the level of the trees
                                  where our voices
                                                      carry off
          beyond the last
                          fragrance of the pines.

          Almost hidden at the top
                              is a hut among thinning trees –
          no one there yet,
                          though in the corner,
                                          a poem,
          ideograms,
                        characters stacked in the air,
                                              and arms

swimming up,
        bodies climbing
                the first rung
                    of clouds.

        for Gary Young

A PAIR OF SHOES

Vincent van Gogh, 1886

Een Paar Schoenen,
the unspeakable
phrases of shoes,
heavy as the dead
history of the ox.
　　　　What obvious
emblems of loss — unlaced
and let go, the spirit from
the body, the bones and
flesh hard with an impaired
glow, a dim grease, soles
split, tops crushed, fallen
back.... They look burnt,
these slouched witnesses,
these blunt badges of
the Republic of the
dispossessed.
　　　　The elemental
apparatus of the lowest
angels, fallen to earth
and left to struggle
in the air, in the rain,
which was the point
of a sorrowful ministry —
these poorest of wings
or what wings come to,
bent, bruised, beneath
the sallow atmosphere,
uttering their last syllables
of rest.
　　　　No matter what
language, this is not

about choice or facility,
not about invention.
This is only potatoes,
two of them pushed
at you on a tin plate
for every meal,
if you're lucky.
And if you are,
if there is a heaven
for anyone, it's dull
yellow with dark spaces
scuffed from stars —
and this is how
you get there.

POEM FREELY ACCEPTED FROM THE POLISH

In the old masters' landscape
the trees have roots beneath
the oil paint...
— Wislawa Szymborska

We are not so badly off if we can
Admire Dutch Painting....
... those trees outside the window, which probably exist...
— Czeslaw Milosz

We could do worse than walk through the representational
    world, praising the common daylight

the least of us deserves – or its lucid and frank
    enunciation in pen and ink with

objective air and space for the trees of the old world
    to come to order beside the cornfield

and river, beneath a horizon brazed, frayed with grist,
    the progress of a windmill or two

dissolving into afternoon, a linen-colored sail
    up stream. How much could it hurt

to admire the unacknowledged principles of trees,
    their metaphorical fortitudes upheld?

And couldn't it well be Philips Koninck himself,
    the obscure Dutch artist, pausing

on the path there to pencil himself in forever, nothing
    at that moment more important

than the little hymn of dust seasoning everything
     on our behalf, setting the world

forth in a brown wash – and in his black hat and habit
     appraising the elms around Rotterdam

set against the defeated landscape, thin-winged against
     the sky as they easily outlive us....

*

In Kew Gardens it was clear that they outshine us –
     cedar of Lebanon, green as the deep sea's

dream, slick with the pewter sun, 235 years already
     matriculated in the blue, and no worries

yet – the ash and false acacia, atlas cedar in its jade –
     bristle sheen. Where beyond the present

did I suppose I was going that morning the rain
     arrived with its brief memoranda and

a thousand small reproaches for idleness, the dull silt
     of over contemplation? Whatever

I thought I was called to do was no clearer than
     the dusty windshield, the *basso profundo*

of the ocean and fog, grey fish bumping in the tides.
     I think God knows I'm not kidding around

anymore, no matter what useless things I've prayed for
     or praised – I should be satisfied

with all the cilia of light just stirring back and forth,
        up from unlit roots to the feathery arms,

even the white cactus flowers breaking out like
        the tide on the night sea to briefly defy

the old saying – *Darkness, Darkness* – covering
        the borderlands of memory where we

already had everything we would ever need, where
        so many leaves cover the ground....

And that sense of hope? It was replaced with middle age –
        with a realistic longing for something

you can no longer name in your bones. The sky
        overlooking us with our unfulfilled

fable where the first one on the Neolithic plain
        holds up a rock, or fire in his hand

to defend a few ferns and poplars at the edge of a pool
        or field, where grain was scattered

unspecified as the stars, where we beheld the great
        bodies of the great beasts in blood

and berry juice, in charcoal and sulfur on the cold
        cave walls. Once we wanted so little

from the light and were appeased with our inelegant
        equations in the night, with our simple

misunderstanding of the relative theories, the special
        interests in the universe. We had faith

in the invisible litany of oak leaves, smoke in wind,
      the starry Sanskrit of an older firmament,

the fragrance of mint or coriander winding through
      the halls. I will not pray against

the vicissitudes again, whatever they might be, however
      many more steps into the air....

*

In the yard this morning a gold finch and great
      western grackle in the bottlebrush,

a scarlet tanager with his brick red head and road sign
      yellow and black, perusing the blooming

jacaranda, the dust–gold silk tree. We will lean out
      a long time toward the sun, with the sea

cataloguing the green past, with our coats on hangers,
      with our slouch like clouds billowing

in the shoulders, of course, and the eucalyptus grove
      in sepia, the amber leaves, the fall

air rusting, the afternoon rich with the apprehensions
      of death in the castor bean. We will rise

or fall within easy sight of the angels, and it will
      surprise no one now when I say

I have no new feelings about God who I no longer
      believe is hiding above the golden

sycamores as I did as a boy, netting shining tadpoles
in the creek and placing them in a jar

to release another day. All things said and done,
I feel as if all things might well be

said and done. But here I am taking in the air
in the park above the cliffs again,

more or less equivalent to the trees, reading our
best poets, realizing I've not had two

original bits of wisdom on all those slips of paper
stuffed in one coat pocket or another.

This is not modesty. These days, even an old song
on the radio can wreck your heart.

Sunlight shifts through the boughs as you begin
to turn over what-in-the-world

it's added up to all this time? And even with dust
in your mouth, you have fifty ways

to say, I fear death more than most, and have hidden
it among the breathing leaves,

or wrapped it in the breakers along the shore in return
for nothing. This is not philosophy —

my blood tastes of the sea, the salt of the white ash
of time and light going forward, heartless

in a few lines. Somewhere toward the back, I've been
content singing my small devotion

to light, and to the birds that carry their part of it
        through the sky, and who hasn't

thought of that? And how much do the trees really ask
        of us after all? I hold my arms out,

reading my book, like the rest seated before the concert
        and string arrangements of the leaves.

So long at the level of the trees – a poem seeming another
        instance of unaccomplished love.

POEM AFTER LU YU

I've been reading the Chinese again, and
    there is still everything
        to steal from –

the entire world, whenever you have time
    to put down your bundle of sticks...
        a hundred themes like

thin clouds drifting by, christened by the moon....
    Boughs of the mimosas move
        with all the improbable

weight of the invisible, but I have my thoughts,
    and space is endless. The empty
        wine bottles squint

with starlight, the usual troubles evaporate.
    The business of heaven blows by
        out there, and from this

vantage point, is the business of heaven,
    out there... And so my company is
        again a few despondent

clouds – unlike water though, the days sail off
    and do not circle back – such
        pity for the years

which come and go in the open window
    with a light breeze, with the ancient
        poet's lines recalling

his boyhood in Yen Chao. Hundreds of years and
half the world between us, but what
are the differences now?

Already I am lonely with the old dust and bitterness
of the silver river-thin clouds drifting by,
christened by the moon...

III.

DESERT SONG, AT 52

By now, I know the obligations
                           of wind —
                                     steadily,
if randomly, unknotting
                   the infinitesimal
                                      strings
of the flesh —
           all the invisible
                          retractions adding up
eventually
          to nothing.
                     Finally, I have taken contentment
upon my back
           and walked out over the hills,
                                         too late
for the vestiges
             of unadorned wisdom,
                              improbable,
in the old and immutable
                   language of light
                                     almost lost
to us beyond the palms.

               I look into the dark,
                              the small exchange
of stars,
        as if we might someday know
                             how gravity
and the electro-magnetic force
                          were pulled
                                     apart
like a milkweed pod

                    bursting out on air,
                                        and somehow all
the bright seeds
                    were charged to realign
                                        themselves
back into that first
                    dense fold.

                                For so long
all we required
                    was a little brilliance
                                pitched across
the sky
                    to focus our abstract
                                inclinations
and assure us that the small
                    ghost ship of the soul
                                        would float
and sail free
                    into this first realm....
                                        We were nothing
to begin,
                    and will end as light —
                                those first particles
in their loneliness
                    are all of us.
                                But perhaps
there is still
                    some misunderstanding,
                                some dim conceptual cargo
that will come
                    back around
                                and redeem us beyond
the dark?
                    If I am middle-aged

                              I will live to 104 —
what would then be
                    the uses
                              of the mind
against the logic of sand,
                         against the molecular
                                        deconstruction
of desire?
          Here, a few clouds bump
                              off course,
a few green leftovers
                 abandoned by
                         an ancient sea
tell us nothing.
               As far as I am
                              concerned,
this is the hard edge
               of the universe
                         where mountains break
down grain by grain,
               where I
                         try to order
thoughts
          like a few of the wind's
                              random notes,
like dry sage leaves
               blowing nowhere
                         across the Mojave....

PHILOSOPHICAL POEM ON THE USUAL SUBJECTS

*I don't need to write memos and letters every
morning. Others will take over, always with
the same hope, the one we know is senseless
and devote our lives to.*
                                        — Milosz

The stars come slowly out as if someone were calling them
                    by name into the sky – surely

We are as essential as the stars? And as lonely. And for their part
                    the trees contribute nothing new –

Though on any given night they seem to read our thoughts
                    before the apparently empty sky.

Nonetheless, there's often something singing above us –
                    dry wind in the olive leaves, only

September and three fires already in the chaparral; wind
                    chorusing in the flames as well, ash

Floating out to sea and back again, like guilt, like pride.
                    I understand that, having taught

Greek tragedy M & W at 3:00 – the burnished stanzas
                    of suffering glimmering briefly

Like October leaves – God, Fate, what-have-you – an allegory
                    with which to face those stars.

For good measure, I sometimes mix in a theory about the collapse
                    of the universe. Some thin clouds

Cast shadows over the geraniums — a suggestion of an afterlife,
             compelling as any. What have I been

Up to all these years, searching for a trap door in the blue,
             the soul I left disguised among

The shining trees of childhood, in the foam off ocean waves —
             every road you can never take again?

                              *

My blood knows the insinuations of salt, a sea tugging at my
             shirt sleeve. I could retire

In the elements, dispassionate as air, little more than the salt-
             colored clouds lifted back to sea—

Our interpretations of events having passed through our porous brains,
             turning us like flowers for the light

When we are done worrying about our molecules colliding and
             starlight ending it all in the cold

Conundrum of space. Above the clouds, all the resolutions
             are walking without shoes.

                              *

The clouds of the 20th century are gone — so much for my inheritance.
             Make what you will of them, where else

Do we resemble the infinite? Fog is the likely interpretation of the past.
             I'm left with the white collar

Around the hills – and the hills broken down like old shoes at the edges –
                    such dog loneliness as there is

Beneath the yellow camphor boughs. You're over 50, you're going
                    to die. With so much sand in those shoes

Who can remember back to the angels we first were? No fish-tailing
                    now in that old Chevrolet, the bent wings

Of its tail fins cutting across the back road home and bouncing you,
                    without a bruise, off the sycamores.

No point now in being clever? What shall we compare life to today?
                    The old coat, the shoe, the onion as emblem

Of the soul? The trees have nothing but themselves; a net of sunlight
                    drags the bottom of a pool and I suppose

It should not matter that nothing rises to the surface. So it is
                    with Desire, the considered imagery

Of our lives. So it is with Hope, that small bird sleeping in my chest,
                    its obscure, incontestable song.

FIVE DAYS RAIN

Just keep thinkin' Butch, that's what you're good at.
— The Sundance Kid

Another cloudburst afternoon with the old sky,
    the new sky, washing away....

Still years from retirement, but I'm thinking
    of the life I might have had

As a theoretical physicist – except the background,
    some facility in math & science,

I had everything it takes... forget the sheets of rain
    falling like a shredded Bible, the past,

The leaves choking the drainpipes, so many soggy facts.
    I need to understand the sea's

Galactic heart, its soft equilibrium – I've been the dreamer
    who's seen it shining effortlessly

Beyond death, beyond the as yet unseen particles,
    the additional dimensions.

The universe is conceivably a horseshoe, a flip-flop or
    knot of strings, a loop-de-loop, a mesh

Of time riding blind on its own back – I could
    have come up with that, no sweat.

Einstein daily thought his way out of his socks,
    usually got it right the first time

With gravity and the big laws of light, and didn't
    even show all his work.

Now they've slowed the speed of light with a deeper than
    deep-freeze freeze; and the physics

All fail once things get smaller than an atom, but who's
    going there? Who needs neutrinos?

They pass right through us, attached to nothing –
    expendable extras discarded

A few seconds after it all really got going. It seems
    you make it up as you go, and

None of us here long enough to prove things otherwise.
    Nonetheless, I think this is where

My talents truly lie – all the rain adding up to
    the invisible, pulling drops along,

Down to us, into earth, angels descending a glass
    ladder, dissolving into thin air . . . .

*

Here, the low mountains rise into clouds, clouds
    I've seen arranged like pillows

Beneath the bare feet of saints as they lifted off
    from the world in their grey robes

No longer weighed down by their molecules, and
    we're to take it all on faith. And so

It's the theory of emptiness that concerns me,
    where the mind goes in the end

When it's no longer even dust? Once I stood
    at Punta Prima, salt spray and wind,

Asking something predictably momentous of the sea,
    and it rolled on in its indolence

And uncertainty, and so I had my vast answer
    and strolled the emptied streets

in Menorca – everyone else dozing, or smoking
    on the sofa after lunch –

And discovered there the spatters of light, the solar
    splendor of oil-glazed puddles

In the stone, which was gone in a breath, like pigeons
    scattered by the backfire of a car.

In the plaza I waited for evening, for the pictograms,
    the anarchy of the stars to argue

One way or another across the drab grids of the mind –
    shimmering like the old tales

Of Paradise. No one is listening any more. I find
    my cats swirled like grey constellations

On the bed, and, as they sleep, catch myself talking
    out loud to them about the world

Losing faith, chasing its own tail. Yet, I imagine
    it's still the same over Paris,

The riverboats of clouds drifting above the boulevards,
    and the nostalgic lives passing

There as if through one grand Gare du Lyon, every
    filigree of wind and sun-polished

Mansard roof in frescoes on the water-blue walls,
    a great gold clock whirring overhead,

Angels from the 18th century riding the amber crest
    of cloud, looking no further than

Montparnasse, all of us staring up at the same sky above –
    so much utter confusion, releasing

For that moment, like pollen from the trees, like rain
    back to its ultimately unseeable source.

PARIS DISPATCH

> *Oh lucky lucky life. Lucky life.*
> — Gerald Stern

I love a place as obvious as Paris. I'm staying at the *Grand Hotel Jeanne D'Arc* for $60 a night and I know *fin de siècle* bistros with *service compris*. I have an L.L. Bean cotton sport coat the color of the leaves along the *Champs Elysées*. I'm a beige tourist like the rest, and blend in along the river walk. I'm quiet and polite with my 75 words, and everyone still in town in August is nice to me when I say *Merci Madame* the way I was taught in kindergarten from our French nuns, Madame Rose and Madame Adrianne.

I love saying *Boulevard Montparnasse, rue Monge, rue du Faubourg St-Dénis*, and knowing the immediate, vibrant ligatures of the air. 4 years old and I pronounced perfectly phrases *en Français*, was awarded gold and silver stars on my school collar. Who else but the French can pile up so many vowels, such sonorous diphthongs over coffee with milk, can offer the mellifluous directions of the boulevard, or the resplendent assonance of just ordering lunch?

Occasional clouds roll over the afternoon like *boules* the men are pitching in the parks, keeping the swelter down. Only an afterthought of rain around 5:00, just long enough to browse the only English bookstore and come out with the dust.

Almost 8 Francs to a dollar and we are eating *Chaum, Morbier* and *Reblochon* – we're drinking little cups of champagne at the neighborhood bar around the corner from our hotel. Our Metro stop is either St. Paul or Bastille – saints or revolution, this far over 40, it doesn't matter now. Still there's plenty to be said for doing nothing, for paying attention – anonymous beneath the clouds – to the aimless crunch of your shoes over centuries of decomposed granite in the *Tuileries*, over the bridge to *Île St. Louis* or to the *Jardin des Plantes* where the dinosaurs have been up-dated and the flower beds appliqued with saffrons and blues, where the ancient pines and pin oaks loiter at the edges, just off *rue Lacepede* and *rue du Cardinal*

Lemoine.

The first thing off the train in *Gare du Nord* I saw the sun-white domes of *Le Sacre Coeur*, and took off down the wide sidewalks blessed with light, putting one happy foot in front of the other with that expansive feeling that you're going to live forever—and my mind flashed to the cover of *The Red Coal*, that black & white photo of Stern with Gilbert in 1950 – thin and serious among all the Parisians on the generous pavement. Stern, too young, of course to know what he would understand 30 years later about Pound and Williams, about fame and obscurity, about the lesson time teaches you: to love obscurity, attached as it was then to the thin fellow and world-beater-to-be in baggy trousers. Now what wouldn't you give to be, as the old song has it, "young and foolish again..."

And there we were, Veinberg and Santos and me 17 years ago, hoping someday we'd be somebody, thinking how lucky we were to be in Paris with enough in our pockets to survive the fall. I thought of little beyond the lovely trees, shopping at the *fromagerie*, buying lamb and *beaujolais nouveau*, returning our wine bottles to the little shop for 20 *centimes*.

17 years ago on these boulevards thinking about the great poets with Veinberg and Santos, knowing we weren't them, but that at least we had poetry pushing out the long phrases of our breath, breath we could see on autumn mornings as we walked down the promenade in the *Jardin des Plantes* between the barbered sycamores—happy in our old clothes after a night when we almost again did not drink too much after hours at the Dixie Melody, listening in that stone basement to someone as flawless and smoldering as Carmen McRae, and walking out of there to the early sun spiking the sleepless river....

Yesterday, I mailed them sentimental postcards of the autumn trees lining the Seine. I've been waiting 17 years to feel this way again. The pink neon still buzzes outside the Dixie Melody, the sidewalks wide and unending, and our lives, more or less, burning away imperceptibly like the little fragments of smoke from the chestnut vendor's coals. If we're lucky, we'll find ourselves on a street, stopping at a small table and happily ordering an over-priced coffee to watch the world go by a while, knowing there is nothing like it, nothing better, as long as we're here ....

IMPERFECT CONTRITION
Southern California

The prayer of the monk is not perfect until he no longer realizes
himself or the fact that he is praying.
— St. Anthony The Great

Come March and the
          drum roll
                    and tumble
of thunder and hail —
          4 a.m.,
                  the ocean shimmering,
tipped
      and tossing
             its mad white hair....
Raw as I am in this
          rare hour, I am at
the silver window glass
          quivering with wind
where my great grey cat,
          Cecil B.,
has been watching
          with the patience of a prophet
for some imminent
          cataclysm in the dark.
                    Here,
where the agapanthus
          and star lilies
                lift up their throats
I, too, stand
        and give thanks
             for my breath reclaimed
from the dry froth

and knots of dream,
                                    back
from the sea–green sheet
                        of the sea,
slick-eyed to the sun,
                        heart crimped, damp
with the rock-dark past –
                        my mind
part of the star pollen
                        dissolving
                                    into dawn....

I stretch my sore bones out,
                        no more
                                    than sun-
bleached sticks of creosote
                        rolled by the mesa gusts –
there is a voice
                out there
                        in the burning manzanita,
in the stellar bits
                so why not
                                    some stanzas
that accommodate
                        the unlikely imposition of meaning
outside any good
                it might ever do us on earth....

In the arroyo,
                something has arrived to save the aloe vera,

the agave petitioning the blue –
                        something gives us this day,
my cat with the full

red fruit of his heart,

                      quick

to praise the least

        morsel

              descended from the air....

The switch for the universe has been thrown,

                      there is no shortage

of power out there,

        and finally, standing here

on a cliff,

      I, too, am

           stiff driftwood,

spinning arms

        holding onto everything

the wind misremembers.

        We have been given everything,

and, God help me,

        I should be able

           to get through this life

without making poems,

        with or without

          the spare

hosannas of rain....

SKY

My distinguishing marks
Are wonder and despair.

—Wislawa Szymborska

What is it with the crows up there –
Complaining about us every day since
That first morning when, once the chemicals
Cooled and the color blue was decided upon,

We crawled out from under the sea
Raising our hands up with the hymn
Of oxygen? Space within space –
Like the sea. But there is nowhere

To grasp a blue bit of it, although
It's in my mind, clear and immeasurable
Despite night regularly rolling down
Its shutter and calling in the birds

Who sing because the thimbles
Of their lungs burn with the white
Idea of it, because it is the magnetic
Fabric of their minds, and leads them,

By the silver tide, home. Is it only
A wide opening to itself –the dis-
Associative atmosphere of the soul;
Where else does the incomplete sentence

Of the future end? No one in this thin
Caplet, at this faint edge, knows
Who's breathing outside the limits
Of our thought, which is to say

The universe is the way Aristarcus of Samos
Saw it one day looking out his window,
Eating a biscuit, when he was the first
To say the earth revolved about the sun

And it got him nowhere. So although
I look out via the interstellar photos
Into the original fires, where is it going
To get me when I want one more day

Of breathing along side the eucalyptus
And sage? Cave of air, all the estimations
Are flung up there and floating, like
Pollen, like shreds of cloud spread over

The horizon, the way my book reports
Flew out of my folder in 1959 as I raced
My bike down San Ysidro Road. Since then,
Little has been clear. So far as I can see,

The trees are always unequal to the stars,
The Pacific coast is the edge of the world.
More each evening now, facing out to the light,
I feel the great blind motion behind the air.

CLOUD JOURNAL

I am growing old making lists of clouds-listening to the dark
        enchantments of the trees, the light-filled assumptions
        of the world finding their way over the horizon line....

But worse things could happen. A North wind could settle
        in your shoulder where the doctor injects an icy cloud
        of crystals to freeze the inflammation – the pain,
        over time, skipping a beat, trailing along bone to
        bone, sharp white spark by spark where you
        misplaced your heart's first obsessions.

Keeping track, I have taken to collecting fountain pens, more
        than I can use in a week. God help me, they almost
        make me happy. I go about in my days recalling the blue
        loops and billows of my name sprawled across the cloud –
        white binder paper of 1959, afternoons when I could still
        toss a football 50 yards, spinning down out of the sky.

Our reports then, were written only with Sheaffer cartridge pens
        bought from the school supply store – the plastic body
        opaque as a marine layer of fog, as our venial and
        parochial souls, the chrome metal cap, colder than that air.

I practiced the Palmer Method of circles and hoops, barrels and
        a smoky locomotive scrawl flowing from my notebook,
        wayward across my desk and out the high transom windows
        silted with a grey strained light until the long pole unhooked
        them to the sky, and we could see the cloud tops reaching
        over the mountain and puffing up at their ends as the sea
        breezes held them back, each tufted like a capital **S**....

I copied out names: Nimbo stratus, Cirro-cumulus, the Cirrus uncinus
    shaped like commas, and Cirrostratus nebulosus, Cirrus fibratus –
    the lost names of angels we never saw. Banks and strips
    wavered overhead like the under-exposed film of heaven.

Later, scratchy black and white prints of a cloud chamber –
    a 42 million electron X-ray volt creating a positron in argon
    gas, a magnetic field torquing the particles into spirals
    and semi spheres, into transient curves and wing shapes,
    clockwise and counter-clockwise, exiting high right....

This was the vague stuff all stuff was made of, the cyclones that spun
    out all the visible and almost invisible, the knowledge of which
    has not made a single thing clearer about the soul.

Looking up all these days, I never completed my list, and I've lost
    hold equally of my inventory of failures of desire, those dark
    clouds clinging perpetually to the underside of heaven, all
    that rain that made my feet heavy on the earth.

But it's not over and done with yet, not all gone to hell in a hand basket,
    and by now I should know a vague thing or two, neither of which
    add up to anything... and that seems to be the main thing
    to know. Like everyone else, I'd seen God, riding the clouds
    in violet frescoes, grey finger stretching out like a streak
    of lightening to Adam, like the X-ray volt – everything floating,
    grey, and representational....

Evidently I, too, was meant to float-with my inconsequential views,
    my incomplete angle on the sky, my lines comfortably
    praising the little it makes me almost content to praise....

But 30 years should come to more than imagery, the equivalency
of clouds – dramatic at times, fibrous and feathery, barely visible
at others – such weathers as were of only passing significance
to most, that meant practically everything to me.

Evanescent or palpable – porcelain, fish bone, or smoke – in the end,
and for all appearances, it looks as if we begin drifting back
across the sky to God, begging for another body....

PHYSICS & THE SECRET OF NOTHING

As a child I drove my father to distraction,
                                    pestering him
no end
        about the nature
                                of a thousand things.
The air is space, right?
                                We live in space don't we?
Then why does the air end
                                somewhere out there above us?

He said
        he would be thankful
                                when I was old
enough to study physics in school –
                                having no idea then
that any grasp of math
                                was light-years beyond
either side of my brain....

                        *

It's always
        right in front of us –
                                sky-like.
Our task is to see things
                                at a grass-blade level
so we might feel
                                the dilemma
                                expanding the air,
the immediate boundaries
                                wherein we must tempt
meaning

with the insignificance
                                of our bones.
Once, compassion almost sufficed
                                and then
we had the sympathy of angels
                                in starry tide pools,
among the spindrift molecules.

                        Who dreamed us up
in three dimensions
                        without knowledge
                                        of the skies,
beneath which you can fill your arms
                                with dry leaves
and like prayer
                        send them
                                        once more skyward?
Sweetly, sweetly
                        the weak font
                                of faith,
the nostalgia of smoke
                        stretches forward.
There in the night,
                        and at the heart of it for us
the one revelation
                        of the moon
                                        beyond the reach
of the magnolia
                        forever.

                                *

The salt–white moon
                        poured into the sea,
                                        sending out circles

to the shore,
        and the Spanish palms
                were talking
in their sleep.
        I could hear the air pick up
around my ears
        as the horizon framed
                a shifting
paradigm of birds,
        and I solved
                the 100 permutations
of the clouds,
        I interpreted a catalog
                of nothing to come....

Space still stretching away
        and truly,
                now and forever,
the world is largely kept away,
        the dove-colored rain hangs
in the boughs,
        and the wind catches
                its breath
and comes back for more.
        I stop to listen.
                I know only that
I mean to be here,
        am sure
        of little more
                than the sky clicking
into place
        again with winter,
                the early sun burning
into the sea,
        freeing

the eucalyptus and acacia leaves
that go up red and gold
and grey
like flames
that sealed
the gates of Eden.

About the Author

Christopher Buckley has published thirteen books of poetry, most recently, *Closer to Home* (2003), and *Star Apocrypha* (2001). For his poetry he has received four Pushcart Prizes, two awards from the Poetry Society of America, a Fulbright Award in Creative Writing to the former Yugoslavia, and is the recipient of NEA grants in poetry for 2001 and 1984.

With Gary Young, Buckley is the editor of *The Geography of Home: California's Poetry of Place* (Hey Day Books, 1999), and with David Oliveira and M.L. Williams he is editor of *How Much Earth: The Fresno Poets* (The Round House Press, 2001). For the University of Michigan Press' Under Discussion series, he has edited *The Poetry of Philip Levine: Stranger to Nothing*, 1991.

Recently he has edited, with Alexander Long, *A Condition of the Spirit: The Life and Work of Larry Levis*, Eastern Washington University Press, 2004.

He has also published *Appreciations: Selected Reviews, Views, & Interviews* (2001), and a book of creative nonfiction, *Cruising State: Growing Up in Southern California* (1994).